MY FIRST
POCKET
GUIDE

DESERT
LIFE

Text/Consultant: Terence Lindsey
Illustrator: David Kirshner

Published by
The National Geographic Society
Reg Murphy, President and Chief Executive Officer
Gilbert Grosvenor, Chairman of the Board
Nina D. Hoffman, Senior Vice President
William R. Gray, Vice President and Director, Book Division
Barbara Lalicki, Director of Children's Publishing
Barbara Brownell, Senior Editor
Mark A. Caraluzzi, Marketing Manager
Vincent P. Ryan, Manufacturing Manager

Library of Congress Catalog Number: 96-0688-52
ISBN: 0-7922-3451-0

Produced for the National Geographic Society by Weldon Owen Pty Ltd
43 Victoria Street, McMahons Point, NSW 2060, Australia
A member of the Weldon Owen Group of Companies
Sydney • San Francisco

President: John Owen
Publisher: Sheena Coupe
Project Editor: Jenni Bruce
Text Editor: Robert Coupe
Assistant Editor: Elizabeth Connolly
Art Director: Sue Burk
Designer: Mark Thacker
Photo Researcher: Amanda Weir
Production Manager: Caroline Webber

Film produced by Mandarin Offset
Printed in Mexico

MY FIRST
POCKET
GUIDE

DESERT LIFE

TERENCE LINDSEY

NATIONAL
GEOGRAPHIC
SOCIETY

INTRODUCTION

Deserts are places where it rarely rains. During the day it is very hot, but nights are often cold, or even frosty. In sandy or stony deserts, the ground is bare and there are few plants. Other deserts, though, may have cactus forests, scrublands with grasses and bushes, or woodlands with some trees.

The deserts of North America are in the Southwest. Much of Mexico is desert, and the states of Oregon, California, Nevada, Utah, Arizona, New Mexico, and Texas all contain large desert areas.

Animals of many kinds live in deserts. Some, such as the roadrunner, seldom live anywhere else. A few are common in other places as well—the coyote, for example, also lives in mountains, grasslands, and even towns and cities.

Many desert animals avoid the hot sun during the day and come out at night to look for food. The best time to see them is at dusk, or very early

in the
morning.
Even if you don't
see them, you can often
find where they have been
the night before by looking in the
sand or dust for their tracks.

HOW TO USE THIS BOOK

This book is organized by type of animal.
First come invertebrates, or animals that
do not have backbones—such as scorpions
and moths. They are followed on page 12
by vertebrates, or animals that do have
backbones—reptiles, amphibians, birds, and
mammals. Each spread helps you to identify
one kind of desert animal. It tells you about
the animal's color, appearance, behavior,
and size. Use the ruler on the inside back
cover to check how long the animal is. A
shaded map of North America shows where
to find the animal, and you can discover an
unusual fact in the "Field Notes." If you
come across a word you don't know, look
it up in the Glossary on page 76.

SCORPION

A scorpion hunts at night, using the stinger at the end of its long, curled tail to kill insects and spiders. While they are out searching for food, scorpions are often eaten by owls and bats.

WHERE TO FIND:
You are most likely to find scorpions in sandy or stony deserts. But be careful—some have a deadly sting!

WHAT TO LOOK FOR:

* **SIZE**
Many scorpions are only an inch long, but some are as long as four inches.

* **COLOR**
Scorpions can be black, brown, or sandy gray.

* **BEHAVIOR**
They hide under rocks during the day and come out at night to hunt.

* **MORE**
Scorpions are not spiders, but like spiders they have eight legs.

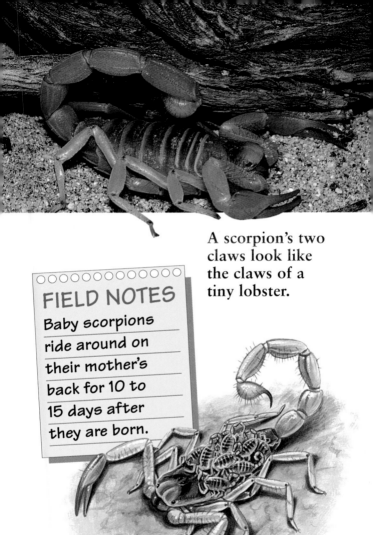

A scorpion's two claws look like the claws of a tiny lobster.

TARANTULA

The long-legged, furry-looking tarantula (tuh-RANCH-uh-luh) is one of the largest spiders in the world. Its poisonous fangs look like tiny pickaxes and are bigger than the fangs of other spiders.

FIELD NOTES

If something disturbs a tarantula, it may rear up and look fierce and aggressive.

A tarantula's body and legs are covered in hair.

WHERE TO FIND:
Tarantulas live mainly on the ground in deserts. They hide under rocks or pieces of bark during the day.

WHAT TO LOOK FOR:

✳ SIZE
With its legs outstretched, a tarantula could cover a grown-up person's hand.

✳ COLOR
Many kinds are brown and black, but some are plain brown, black, or gray.

✳ BEHAVIOR
Tarantulas use their fangs to kill insects, lizards, and even mice.

✳ MORE
Their bite is dangerous, but they rarely bite people.

YUCCA MOTH

The yucca (YUCK-uh) moth lays its eggs in a yucca plant's flowers, which turn into seedpods with the eggs inside. When the eggs hatch, the caterpillars eat the seeds until they are big enough to bore their way out.

Birds find yucca moths hard to see against the white flowers of the yucca plant.

WHERE TO FIND:
Look for yucca moths near yucca plants that are in flower. Yucca plants grow mainly in deserts.

WHAT TO LOOK FOR:

✳ SIZE
From wingtip to wingtip, this moth is a little more than an inch wide.

✳ COLOR
The yucca moth is white.

✳ BEHAVIOR
It is active at night, when the scent of the yucca flowers is strong and attractive.

✳ MORE
As they visit yucca plants, yucca moths carry pollen from one flower to another. This helps the plants to grow seeds.

FIELD NOTES
All moths' eggs hatch into caterpillars that will eventually turn into moths.

DESERT TORTOISE

 During the hottest part of the day, a desert tortoise shelters in its underground burrow. It comes out in the early morning and late afternoon to feed on any grasses or other plants it can find.

WHERE TO FIND:
Desert tortoises live in very dry places where scrub and cactuses grow. They like the floors of canyons.

WHAT TO LOOK FOR:

✳ **SIZE**
They grow about 14 inches long.

✳ **COLOR**
Their shells are mainly dull brown and often have small red markings.

✳ **BEHAVIOR**
Sometimes, several desert tortoises spend winter in the same burrow.

✳ **MORE**
They get all the moisture they need from the plants they eat, but will drink water if they find it.

Desert tortoises eat many types of plants, including cactus fruits.

FIELD NOTES

Males fight for territory by charging at each other and colliding chest to chest.

DESERT IGUANA

As soon as it senses danger, a desert iguana (i-GWAHN-uh) scuttles away to hide in the nearest burrow. This lizard will try to scare other desert iguanas away from its territory by doing push-ups and bobbing its head.

FIELD NOTES

On hot days, desert iguanas often climb into bushes, where the air is cooler than on the ground.

You can tell a desert iguana by the crest of small scales along its back.

WHERE TO FIND:

The desert iguana lives in rocky or sandy areas in deserts. Look for it where thorn scrub grows.

WHAT TO LOOK FOR:

✳ SIZE
It is between 10 and 16 inches long.

✳ COLOR
This grayish brown lizard has pale spots on its body and dark spots on its tail.

✳ BEHAVIOR
The leaves of creosote (KREE-uh-soat) bushes are this iguana's favorite food, but it sometimes eats insects.

✳ MORE
A female lays between three and eight dull white eggs at a time.

15

FRINGE-TOED LIZARD

 If frightened, a fringe-toed lizard will scurry across a dune and then suddenly dive under the sand. The fringes on its toes keep it from sinking into loose sand as it runs.

WHERE TO FIND:
You are most likely to see fringe-toed lizards on sand dunes and other open areas of bare sand.

WHAT TO LOOK FOR:

✳ SIZE
Fringe-toed lizards can measure up to seven inches—about as long as a pencil.

✳ COLOR
They are very pale gray with small markings of darker gray.

✳ BEHAVIOR
They eat small insects and spiders.

✳ MORE
To tell enemies it has seen them, this lizard raises its tail and displays the black and white bands on the underside.

Notice the fringes of pointed scales on this lizard's toes.

FIELD NOTES

Overlapping eyelids, flapped nostrils, and ridges over the lizard's ears and eyes help to keep sand out.

CHUCKWALLA

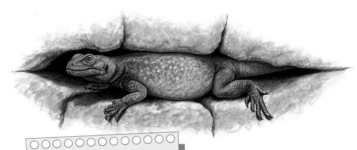

Like many other lizards, a chuckwalla (chuhk-WAHL-uh) basks in the sun for an hour or two every morning. Once its body has warmed up, it can move around and look for flowers and fruit to eat.

FIELD NOTES

A frightened chuckwalla may enter a crevice and puff itself up with air until it fits tightly.

A chuckwalla has loose folds of skin around its neck and along its sides.

WHAT TO LOOK FOR:

✳ SIZE
An old male can be 17 inches long, but females and youngsters are smaller.

✳ COLOR
Most chuckwallas are blackish or grayish on the head and body and a paler color on the tail.

✳ BEHAVIOR
A male mates with several females.

✳ MORE
A female chuckwalla lays between five and ten eggs at a time.

COLLARED LIZARD

When two male collared lizards fight over territory, they face each other and bob their heads up and down. If neither lizard gives up, they will wrestle until one runs away.

WHERE TO FIND:
Look for collared lizards on hot, dry, stony hillsides where there are large, flat rocks for basking.

WHAT TO LOOK FOR:

✳ SIZE
They are between 8 and 16 inches long.

✳ COLOR
They can be different colors, but are often bright blue and yellow.

✳ BEHAVIOR
A collared lizard eats mainly insects. It may also eat smaller lizards.

✳ MORE
Males always have two black circles, or "collars," around their necks. Females often have red spots along their sides.

This collared lizard is standing up on all four legs to let cool air pass under its body.

FIELD NOTES

When frightened, this lizard raises its head and tail and runs on its back legs.

TEXAS HORNED LIZARD

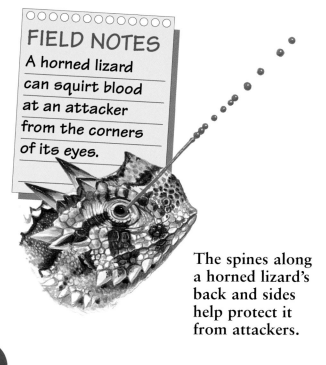

You could easily miss seeing a Texas horned lizard because it blends in well with its background. Instead of running away from an enemy, this lizard will stay still, hiss loudly, and threaten to bite.

FIELD NOTES

A horned lizard can squirt blood at an attacker from the corners of its eyes.

The spines along a horned lizard's back and sides help protect it from attackers.

WHERE TO FIND:
They live in deserts and grasslands in many states, including Texas. They like patches of sand or gravel.

WHAT TO LOOK FOR:

✳ SIZE
Texas horned lizards are between three and seven inches long.

✳ COLOR
Their mottled coloring can include gray, tan, reddish brown, or brown.

✳ BEHAVIOR
Active in the daytime, they often sleep in burrows at night.

✳ MORE
A horned lizard will stand over a line of ants and eat them as they pass by.

BANDED GECKO

 Because it can see in the dark, a banded gecko can hunt insects and spiders at night. During the day, it shelters from the sun in rock crevices or under dead branches on the ground.

WHERE TO FIND:
They live in canyons, rocky hillsides, and sand dunes in deserts. You can often see them on roads at night.

WHAT TO LOOK FOR:

✴ SIZE
A banded gecko can be six inches long.

✴ COLOR
It is mainly brownish pink with dark brown and yellow bands along its back.

✴ BEHAVIOR
If you pick up a banded gecko, it will make a chirping noise.

✴ MORE
Unlike most geckos, the banded gecko has eyelids, but it still cleans its eyes with its tongue as other geckos do.

Geckos do not have scales,
but their skin is rough,
like soft sandpaper.

FIELD NOTES

A gecko's tail will
break off if an
attacker, such as
a ringtail, grabs it.
The gecko later
grows a new tail.

GILA MONSTER

The world has only two poisonous lizards, and the gila (HEE-luh) monster is one of them. It catches small birds, mice, and other lizards in its teeth and poisons them as it slowly chews them.

FIELD NOTES

Gila monsters store fat in their tails. They can live on this fat when food is hard to find.

The scales of a gila monster are rounded like little beads.

WHERE TO FIND:
Gila monsters live in sandy or stony deserts, especially near water holes or thickets. They often rest under rocks.

WHAT TO LOOK FOR:

✳ **SIZE**
These lizards grow nearly two feet long.

✳ **COLOR**
They are black with pink, or sometimes yellow or orange, markings.

✳ **BEHAVIOR**
Females lay from three to five eggs at a time. These hatch in about ten months.

✳ **MORE**
A gila monster's poison comes from glands in its lower jaw. Babies can produce poison as soon as they hatch.

GLOSSY SNAKE

Many snakes have rough scales, but the glossy snake gets its name from its smooth, shiny scales. This snake preys on lizards and small mammals by coiling around them and squeezing them to death.

WHERE TO FIND:
Glossy snakes live in many different places, from woodlands to deserts, but they prefer dry, sandy areas.

WHAT TO LOOK FOR:

✶ SIZE
A glossy snake grows to nearly six feet long—about as long as a man is tall.

✶ COLOR
It is usually pale sandy brown with darker, black-edged blotches.

✶ BEHAVIOR
It spends the day in a burrow and comes out at dusk to hunt on the ground.

✶ MORE
When frightened, a glossy snake quivers the tip of its tail.

The glossy snake has a narrow head with a dark line running from the eye to the jaw.

FIELD NOTES
A female glossy snake lays between 3 and 23 eggs at a time. The eggs hatch after about 10 weeks.

SIDEWINDER

A sidewinder is a kind of rattlesnake that swings its body sideways to move quickly across hot, shifting sand. It hunts at night and can find birds and other prey by sensing the heat of their bodies.

FIELD NOTES

Whenever you visit sandy deserts, look for curved tracks that may have been left by a sidewinder.

The hole beneath each eye is the organ that senses prey in the dark.

WHERE TO FIND:
Sidewinders live mainly in flat desert country, especially where there are very few plants.

WHAT TO LOOK FOR:

✴ SIZE
These snakes grow up to 32 inches long.

✴ COLOR
Their pale sandy brown color and cream, brown, or gray markings make them hard to see against rocks.

✴ BEHAVIOR
During the day, a sidewinder hides in a burrow or another cool, shady place.

✴ MORE
The sidewinder's bite is poisonous and can kill a person.

WESTERN SPADEFOOT

 As long as the weather is rainy, the western spadefoot hunts at night for insects. During dry spells, though, it may stay in its cool, moist burrow for months.

WHERE TO FIND:
Look for western spadefoots in sandy or gravelly soil in desert country, especially during and after rain.

WHAT TO LOOK FOR:

＊SIZE
They grow about three inches long.

＊COLOR
They are mottled gray, brown, or green.

＊BEHAVIOR
Male spadefoots sing as they float in water. Their song is a soft, short trill that sounds a bit like a cat's purring.

＊MORE
When they first hatch, baby spadefoots live underwater and are called tadpoles. They have no arms or legs.

A spadefoot is an amphibian
that uses its spadelike back feet
to burrow backward into loose soil.

When it starts
to rain, a
female comes
out of her burrow
to lay eggs in a
pool of rainwater.

TURKEY VULTURE

In the morning, a turkey vulture basks for a while on a high perch before flying off on warm, rising air. For the rest of the day it soars high aboveground, always on the lookout for food.

The turkey vulture's head is dull red and has no feathers on it.

WHERE TO FIND:
Turkey vultures live in dry, open country, especially deserts, throughout most of North America.

WHAT TO LOOK FOR:

✷ SIZE
Turkey vultures measure a little more than two feet from beak to tail. Their wingspan is almost six feet.

✷ COLOR
Their feathers are dusty black.

✷ BEHAVIOR
As they soar, they spread their wings in a V-shape. They often fly in flocks.

✷ MORE
They feed on dead animals that they find on the ground.

FIELD NOTES

A vulture has very sharp eyesight and can spot food from a great height.

HARRIS'S HAWK

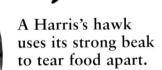 Harris's hawks are sociable birds and often live and hunt in a group. After a pair produces young, others in the group may help find food for the chicks. This lets the group raise more young.

A Harris's hawk uses its strong beak to tear food apart.

FIELD NOTES
When Harris's hawks hunt together, one may chase the prey, while the others wait to pounce.

WHERE TO FIND:
Harris's hawks live in desert regions that have trees or shrubs for nesting. They prefer woods near rivers.

WHAT TO LOOK FOR:

✳ SIZE
A Harris's hawk is about two feet long, with a wingspan of nearly four feet.

✳ COLOR
It is mostly chocolate brown, but has chestnut shoulders and thighs. The tail is white with a broad black band.

✳ BEHAVIOR
This hawk's call is a loud, harsh scream.

✳ MORE
Using sharp, curved claws, a Harris's hawk can get a tight hold on its prey.

SCALED QUAIL

 Even though it can fly, a scaled quail lives almost entirely on the ground. If danger threatens, it prefers to run rather than fly away. This bird must drink every day, so it stays near water holes and streams.

WHERE TO FIND:
Look for scaled quails on flat, stony hilltops or in scrublands. They often visit desert ranches.

WHAT TO LOOK FOR:

✳ **SIZE**
A scaled quail is about ten inches long.

✳ **COLOR**
It is mainly pale grayish brown and has a white topknot on its head.

✳ **BEHAVIOR**
Female scaled quails lay about a dozen eggs in a scrape—a nest on the ground that is lined with dry grass and feathers.

✳ **MORE**
When a scaled quail does fly, its wings make a buzzing, whirring sound.

The neck and chest feathers of a scaled quail look like the scales on a fish.

FIELD NOTES

Scaled quails live mainly in pairs, but in winter, they gather in flocks called coveys.

ROADRUNNER

A roadrunner rarely flies, preferring to race along on its strong legs. This big, brown bird can change direction swiftly, thanks to a very long tail that acts like a rudder. Roadrunners chase and eat scorpions, rattlesnakes, and other small animals.

FIELD NOTES

When chasing a lizard or other prey, a roadrunner can reach a speed of 15, or even 20, miles per hour.

A roadrunner uses its strong, skinny bill for stabbing prey.

WHERE TO FIND:
You may see a roadrunner on the ground in most desert country, especially around cactuses and scrub.

WHAT TO LOOK FOR:

✳ SIZE
From its bill to the tip of its tail, a roadrunner is nearly two feet long.

✳ COLOR
Most of its feathers are brownish gray, streaked with white. Its underside is whitish, with brown streaks on its chest.

✳ BEHAVIOR
Roadrunners live in pairs that stay together all their lives.

✳ MORE
Their song is a moaning *coo-coo-coo*.

ELF OWL

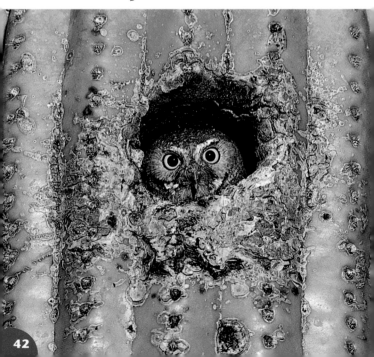

Because elf owls hunt at night, you might catch a glimpse of one at dawn or dusk. But you are more likely to hear the loud calls of this sparrow-size bird. It yelps like a puppy, and whistles and whinnies.

A hole in a saguaro (suh-WAHR-uh) cactus is a favorite place for an elf owl's nest.

WHERE TO FIND:
Elf owls live in desert woodlands and scrublands. Look for them wherever you find saguaro cactuses.

WHAT TO LOOK FOR:

✳ SIZE
At less than six inches long, the elf owl is the smallest owl in North America.

✳ COLOR
This owl is sandy brown, with small gray and dull white markings. It has yellow eyes and white eyebrows.

✳ BEHAVIOR
Elf owls use nest holes that have been abandoned by woodpeckers.

✳ MORE
They eat insects, scorpions, and spiders.

FIELD NOTES

An elf owl grasps an insect in its sharp beak and then carries the prey back to its nest hole.

43

COSTA'S HUMMINGBIRD

 A male Costa's hummingbird attracts a female by zooming before her in a spectacular flight display. This is the only hummingbird that lives in hot, dry deserts.

WHERE TO FIND:
Look for this hummingbird among flowering shrubs, especially cactuses or yucca plants, on desert slopes.

WHAT TO LOOK FOR:

✳ SIZE
Including its slender bill, a Costa's hummingbird is almost four inches long.

✳ COLOR
Males and females have mainly shiny green feathers, with white chests. Males also have purple caps and throats.

✳ BEHAVIOR
Their call is a high, sharp, metallic *tink*.

✳ MORE
Costa's hummingbirds eat insects and drink nectar from flowers.

A hummingbird's wings beat so fast that they make a humming sound.

GILA WOODPECKER

If you hear a sharp, shrill call like *pit!* or *huit!* in a saguaro desert, look up and you may see a gila woodpecker perched high above. When it takes flight, look for the big white patch near the tip of each wing.

A male gila woodpecker has a bright red patch on the top of its head.

WHERE TO FIND:
The gila woodpecker lives mainly in dry scrublands and cactus deserts. It sometimes visits towns.

WHAT TO LOOK FOR:

❋ SIZE
This bird is about nine inches long.

❋ COLOR
Its back and wings have black and white bars. The rest of the bird is sandy brown.

❋ BEHAVIOR
Like other woodpeckers, it finds insects by drilling the bark of trees with its bill.

❋ MORE
Using strong claws, the gila woodpecker clings to the trunks of trees or cactuses. A long, stiff tail helps it stay balanced.

○○○○○○○○○○○○○○
FIELD NOTES
This bird makes a nest for its eggs inside a saguaro cactus. When the babies fly away, it abandons the nest.

PHAINOPEPLA

Phainopeplas (FAY-noe-pep-luhs) love to eat mistletoe berries, but if berries are out of season they will swoop after insects, catching them in flight. In winter months, when they are not nesting, these birds usually travel in flocks of about fifty.

FIELD NOTES

When a male phainopepla is flying, you can see a large white patch on each of its wings.

Like males, females have red eyes and spiky crests.

WHAT TO LOOK FOR:

✻ **SIZE**
They are about eight inches long.

✻ **COLOR**
The male is glossy blue-black. The female is dull brownish gray.

✻ **BEHAVIOR**
The male builds a nest alone. The female lays two or three eggs and sits on them until they hatch.

✻ **MORE**
Their feathers look silky. "Phainopepla" means "shining robe" in Greek.

LE CONTE'S THRASHER

 In the hottest, driest, and barest desert areas, you can often see a Le Conte's thrasher scuttling between clumps of dry bushes, scrabbling about in the sand for insects to eat.

WHERE TO FIND:
Le Conte's thrashers live in deserts where there are scattered bushes. Look for them in dry river beds.

WHAT TO LOOK FOR:

✳ SIZE
These birds are about 11 inches long.

✳ COLOR
They are mainly sandy gray, with whitish chins and buff-colored bellies.

✳ BEHAVIOR
Their most common call is a sharp whistle. They often sing early in the morning or at dusk.

✳ MORE
Because they are not good fliers, they prefer to run away when frightened.

A Le Conte's thrasher has a long, curved bill. Males and females have the same coloring.

○○○○○○○○○○○○○○○○○○

FIELD NOTES

When it runs, a Le Conte's thrasher holds its long, dark tail straight up.

CACTUS WREN

Each year, a cactus wren builds a new nest for its eggs. When the young have flown away, it still sleeps in the nest at night. At any time of day or year, you may hear its *cha-cha-cha-cha-cha* song.

FIELD NOTES

A cactus wren's nest is a bulky, untidy dome of sticks, built in the branches of a cactus or bush.

WHERE TO FIND:
Look and listen for the cactus wren on dry rocky hillsides, especially if there are lots of cactuses.

WHAT TO LOOK FOR:

✳ **SIZE**
At about eight and a half inches long, it is the largest North American wren.

✳ **COLOR**
The cactus wren's back is dark brown, spotted with white. Its buff-colored breast and belly have small black spots.

✳ **BEHAVIOR**
It feeds on the ground and eats insects.

✳ **MORE**
Notice its long, slightly curved bill.

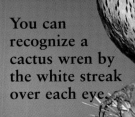

You can recognize a cactus wren by the white streak over each eye.

LONG-NOSED BAT

 At night, long-nosed bats leave their daytime shelters in dark caves or mine shafts. Groups of them fly out far over the desert, feeding on the nectar and fruits of cactuses and other plants.

WHERE TO FIND:
Long-nosed bats often live in caves on mountain slopes near deserts. In winter, they fly south into Mexico.

WHAT TO LOOK FOR:

✳ SIZE
A long-nosed bat grows only about 4 inches long—as long as this page is wide. Its wingspan is about 11 inches.

✳ COLOR
It is covered in brownish gray fur.

✳ BEHAVIOR
As the bat flies from flower to flower, it spreads the pollen of cactus plants.

✳ MORE
The tip of a long-nosed bat's nose sticks up and is shaped like a leaf.

Flying over a cactus flower, a long-nosed bat snatches nectar with a stab of its tongue.

FIELD NOTES

Long-nosed bats live in large groups called colonies. They often groom each other's fur.

RINGTAIL

During the day, ringtails usually sleep in dens, but you may sometimes see one napping in a tree. At night, they come out to hunt, sneaking up on bugs, birds, and small mammals and suddenly pouncing on them.

FIELD NOTES

Ringtails are excellent climbers. They can even leap from tree to tree as they chase their prey.

A ringtail's large, dark eyes help it to find prey at night.

WHERE TO FIND:
Ringtails prefer to live in rocky places with cliffs and ledges. They usually stay near a stream or water hole.

WHAT TO LOOK FOR:

✳ SIZE
Including its tail, a ringtail measures more than two feet.

✳ COLOR
Its body is covered with sandy gray fur. The tail has black and white rings.

✳ BEHAVIOR
Adult ringtails usually live alone. They come together only to have families.

✳ MORE
Their tails help them keep their balance when climbing.

HOG-NOSED SKUNK

Hog-nosed skunks are covered with long fur, except for their bare, piglike snouts. Young skunks stay with their mothers until they grow up. Then they usually live alone in rocky dens at the bottom of cliffs.

FIELD NOTES

A hog-nosed skunk uses its tough snout to dig spiders and snails out of the earth.

A hog-nosed skunk usually looks for food at night.

WHERE TO FIND:
Most hog-nosed skunks live in stony desert country. They like dry scrublands with scattered trees and cactuses.

WHAT TO LOOK FOR:

✳ SIZE
From its snout to the tip of its tail, this skunk can measure up to three feet.

✳ COLOR
Its tail, back, and the top of its head are white. The rest of the animal is black.

✳ BEHAVIOR
It defends itself by spraying a smelly liquid from under its tail. When two skunks fight, they may spray each other.

✳ MORE
A hog-nosed skunk has sharp claws.

COYOTE

Coyotes belong to the dog family. They have learned to live in many different places, from hot deserts and windy plains to snowy mountains. You might even see them in towns and cities.

WHERE TO FIND:
Coyotes live in most parts of North America. In deserts, you are likely to see them in canyons and near thickets.

WHAT TO LOOK FOR:

✳ SIZE
From its nose to the tip of its tail, a coyote can be up to 50 inches long.

✳ COLOR
It is mostly reddish gray with a lighter, buff-colored underside.

✳ BEHAVIOR
Coyotes often live alone, but some live in small groups.

✳ MORE
While running, a coyote usually holds its bushy tail low between its legs.

Even as a pup, a coyote looks a bit like a German shepherd dog.

FIELD NOTES
At night in the desert, you may hear the distant howls, barks, and yelps of coyotes.

SWIFT FOX

The swift fox is named for its speed—it runs as fast as 25 miles per hour. This little fox is also called the kit fox because, just as kittens are smaller than cats, it is much smaller than other foxes.

A swift fox pricks up its ears to listen for prey.

FIELD NOTES

A female raises four to seven cubs in an underground den. The father brings them food.

WHERE TO FIND:
Swift foxes live in deserts or grasslands. They sleep in dens by day and come out at night to hunt.

WHAT TO LOOK FOR:

✳ **SIZE**
The head and body of a swift fox measure a little less than two feet. The bushy tail is almost a foot long.

✳ **COLOR**
A swift fox is mainly gray and reddish brown, with a much paler throat and belly. The tip of its tail is black.

✳ **BEHAVIOR**
It hunts mice and other small mammals.

✳ **MORE**
Big ears give this fox superb hearing.

PECCARY

A peccary (PECK-uh-ree) is a kind of small pig with a pink snout, small hooves, and coarse fur. Peccaries usually feed early or late in the day and will eat almost anything. They especially like to dig up roots.

WHERE TO FIND:
Peccaries live in rocky canyons and scrublands. Look for them near water holes in the desert.

WHAT TO LOOK FOR:

✳ SIZE
Peccaries are about three feet long, and nearly two feet high at the shoulders.

✳ COLOR
Their fur is a mixture of black and gray.

✳ BEHAVIOR
Peccaries usually gather in herds of between 6 and 40 animals.

✳ MORE
They have weak eyesight. Members of a herd keep together by using their sense of smell.

A band of paler fur runs like a collar around a peccary's neck.

PRONGHORN

Sensing danger, a pronghorn—a deerlike animal—will signal to another by fluffing out the white hairs on its rump. Female pronghorns live in herds with their young. Adult males live alone.

The horns of a male, like this one, are larger than a female's.

WHERE TO FIND:
You may see pronghorns in dry, flat, open country where there are grasses and bushes but no trees.

WHAT TO LOOK FOR:

✳ SIZE
An adult pronghorn is about three and a half feet high at the shoulder.

✳ COLOR
It is tan or sandy gray with a white belly and chin and white bands on its throat.

✳ BEHAVIOR
A male pronghorn makes a snorting sound to frighten off an intruder.

✳ MORE
A pronghorn has two horns. Each horn has a hook, or prong, at the front.

DESERT WOOD RAT

Because the desert wood rat often takes things from the backpacks of campers, some people call it the pack rat. This rat makes its large nest mainly from sticks and branches, but it may sometimes add items such as socks and keys.

FIELD NOTES
Desert wood rats usually build their bulky nests beside cactuses, under shrubs, or on rocky ledges.

A wood rat's whiskers act as feelers and help it to find food at night.

WHERE TO FIND:
The desert wood rat likes dry, stony, or rocky hillsides where there are plenty of cactuses and yucca plants.

WHAT TO LOOK FOR:

✴ SIZE
The head and body measure about seven inches. The tail adds another six inches.

✴ COLOR
It is mainly sandy gray, with a pale belly.

✴ BEHAVIOR
This small mammal feeds at night on seeds, berries, and cactuses, holding the food in its paws as it nibbles.

✴ MORE
A wood rat may raise more than four families in a year.

DESERT KANGAROO RAT

 Hopping at high speed, a desert kangaroo rat stays balanced with the help of a long tail. This mammal doesn't need to drink. It makes water inside its body from the seeds it eats.

WHERE TO FIND:

The desert kangaroo rat prefers sandy or scrubby areas. You might see one on a desert road at night.

WHAT TO LOOK FOR:

✳ SIZE
The head and body are about five inches long, but the tail is much longer.

✳ COLOR
It is mainly sandy brown, with a white underside. Its tail has a white tip.

✳ BEHAVIOR
During the day, it shelters in burrows. It comes out at night to feed.

✳ MORE
A desert kangaroo rat has pouches in its mouth for storing food.

FIELD NOTES

Kangaroo rats can run, but they prefer to hop. In a single bound, they can hop two feet.

A kangaroo rat holds food in its small paws and hops on its big feet.

ANTELOPE JACKRABBIT

In a single bound, the antelope jackrabbit can cover more than 20 feet! While running as fast as 35 miles per hour, this large, nimble hare can suddenly change direction to escape a predator such as a coyote.

A jackrabbit's long ears help it to stay cool. Heat from its body flows out through them.

WHERE TO FIND:
The antelope jackrabbit lives in dry grasslands and deserts. You may see one sitting under a shady bush.

WHAT TO LOOK FOR:

✳ **SIZE**
This hare measures about 20 inches.

✳ **COLOR**
It is mainly sandy gray, with a pale belly.

✳ **BEHAVIOR**
Antelope jackrabbits scrape shallow, saucerlike holes, called forms, in the ground and rest in them during the day.

✳ **MORE**
Instead of drinking water, they feed on plants, such as cactuses, that contain lots of moisture.

FIELD NOTES

In spring, males fight. They batter each other with their paws until one runs away.

73

DESERT COTTONTAIL

The desert cottontail doesn't dig its own burrow. Instead, it "borrows" burrows that other animals have made and abandoned. It will run into a burrow, or under a bush, if something frightens it.

FIELD NOTES

When a cottontail runs away, its bouncing "cotton" tail warns other rabbits that danger is near.

With its big ears, a cottontail can hear sounds from all directions.

WHERE TO FIND:
Look for desert cottontails in dry grasslands and brushlands, especially in low-lying places.

WHAT TO LOOK FOR:

✳ SIZE
A large male grows about 15 inches long. Females are a little smaller.

✳ COLOR
A desert cottontail is pale sandy gray.

✳ BEHAVIOR
It is sometimes active in the day, but usually feeds at night. It eats grass, flowers, and the leaves of herbs.

✳ MORE
A desert cottontail will sometimes climb up a sloping tree to rest.

GLOSSARY

bask When an animal lies in the sun to soak up the warmth it needs to move around.

bill A bird's beak.

burrow A hole that an animal digs in the ground for its home.

canyon A deep valley with steep walls.

creosote A kind of low bush that is common in deserts.

crest Feathers that stand up on the heads of some birds.

crevice A small crack in a rock.

den A place where an animal lives.

dusk The time just before it becomes dark at night.

gland A part of the body that makes a substance, such as venom, for the body to use.

mammal A warm-blooded animal, usually with hair or fur, that feeds its young on milk from the mother's body.

mate When an adult male and female come together to produce young.

mottled A pattern in which dark spots are blurred against a paler background.

nectar The sweet fluid made by flowers.

pollen The fine, yellow powder made by flowers so they can reproduce.

prey Any animal hunted by other animals for food.

saguaro A kind of large, treelike cactus.

scrubland A dry area with small bushes and low trees.

soar When a bird flies high without flapping its wings.

song A special kind of call a bird makes to attract a mate or protect its territory.

territory The place where an animal or group of animals lives. Animals defend their territory from other animals of the same kind.

thicket A place where bushes and small trees grow very closely together.

yucca A kind of shrub or tree with spiky leaves and waxy, greenish white flowers.

INDEX OF
DESERT LIFE

ABOUT THE CONSULTANT

Terence Lindsey was born in England and raised and educated in Canada. He has traveled widely in North America, Europe, and Australasia, but has made Australia his home for the past 25 years. His interests encompass most of the natural world. He has studied, written, and taught mainly about birds, with a special interest in avian zoogeography and foraging and reproduction strategies. He is an Associate of the Australian Museum and a former tutor at the University of Sydney, but now devotes most of his time to writing, traveling, and consulting.

PHOTOGRAPHIC CREDITS